A Jodo Shinshu Buddhist

Alphabet Book

浄土真宗
ＡＢＣブック

Text by John & Eri Iwohara

Artwork by Eri Iwohara

Dedication

To Grandparents and their
Grandchildren
&
To Sean and Jean
(who this book was originally
intended for)

A Jodo Shinshu Buddhist Alphabet Book

A is for Amida

アミダ
Amida = 阿弥陀

B is for Buddha

ブッダ
Buddha = 仏

Amida Buddha is always with me!

あみださまは
いつも わたしの
そばに いらっしゃる

C is for Candle

キャンドル
Candle = ろうそく

4

that lights up the way

ひかりは　道を
あかるく　てらす

D is for Dragon

ドラゴン　　りゅう
Dragon = 龍

who can cause a
great rain

りゅうは 雨を ふらす

E is for Elephant

エレファント　　ぞう
Elephant ＝ 象

majestic and bold

ほとけさまは
ぞうの ように
どうどうと している

F is for Flower

フラワー
Flower = 花

that shares its
beauty with all

どの花も みんな
うつくしい

G is for Gong

ゴング
Gong = きん（かね）

that rings
throughout

大きんの　音は
どこまでも　ひびく

H is for Hanamatsuri

ハ ナ マ ツ リ
Hanamatsuri = 花祭り

Happy birthday Sakyamuni Buddha!

４月８日は
「花まつり」
おしゃかさまの
おたんじょう日

I is for Incense

インセンス　こう
Incense = お香

that makes the air
smell so nice

いい かおりは 心を
おちつかせて くれる

J is for Jodo

ジョウド
Jodo = 浄土

the Pure Land of the Buddha

お浄土は
ほとけさまの 国
とても うつくしい
ところ

K is for Kansho

カンショウ
Kansho = 喚鐘

the bell that's rung
7, 5, 3

七回 五回 三回
なったら
みんなで
おまいり しよう

L is for Lotus

ロータス　　れんげ
Lotus ＝ 蓮華（はすの花）

that grows out of
muddy water

はすは
どろの　中から
花が　さく

M is for Music

ミュージック　おんがく
Music ＝ 音楽

that fills the air
when we chant

お経は
音楽の ように
ひびく

N is for Nenju

ネンジュ
Nenju = 念珠

we hold in both hands

両手に　おねんじゅを
かけましょう

O is for Otoki

オトキ
Otoki = お斎

the meal we eat
after service.
Don't forget to say
itadakimasu and
gochisosama!

おまいりの　あとの
ごちそう
「いただきます」
「ごちそうさま」

P is for Prince

プリンス　おうじ
Prince = 王子

Sakyamuni Buddha was a prince of the Sakya

おしゃかさまは
シャカぞくの
王子さま

Q is for Queen Maya

クィーン　マーヤ
Queen Maya = マーヤ夫人

the mother of
Sakyamuni Buddha

マーヤ夫人は
おしゃかさまの
お母さん

R is for Rokuji

ロクジ
Rokuji = 六字

南無阿弥陀仏

Roku is 6 in Japanese. How many Kanji are there in the name Namo Amida Butsu?

「六字」は
南無阿弥陀仏の
六つの字

S is for Shinran Shonin

シンラン　ショウニン
Shinran Shonin = 親鸞聖人

the founder of
Jodo Shinshu

しんらん聖人は
浄土真宗を
ひらいた 人

T is for Taiko

the Japanese drum

たいこが
ドン！ ドン！ ドン！
リズムに のって
ぼんおどり

U is for Uchishiki

ウ チ シ キ
Uchishiki = 打敷

the triangle cloth in
the altar

ほとけさまの 前_{まえ}の
つくえに かける
三角形_{さんかっけい}の きれいな 布_{ぬの}

V is for Vaidehi

ヴァイデヒ　　いだいけぶにん
Vaidehi ＝ 韋提希夫人

a mother who struggled but showed us the truth

おしゃかさまから
たすけられた
あじゃせ王子の
お母さん

W is for Wheel

ウイール　ほうりん
(Dharma) Wheel = 法輪

count the spokes!
How many do we
have?

ほうりんは
ほとけさまの 教えを
あらわす

X is in the word excellent

エクセレント
Excellent = すぐれている

it is a word used with rare to describe the Buddha's Wisdom and Compassion!

Can you find the "x" in excellent?

ほとけさまは

い　ち　ば　ん
一番 すぐれた

ちえと　じひを

もっている

Y is for Yoraku

ヨウラク
Yoraku = 瓔珞

a necklace of precious stone. Can you find the yoraku in the Onaijin?

ようらくは

お浄土の うつくしい

おかざり

おないじんの どこに

あるかな

Z is for Zenchishiki

ゼンチシキ
Zenchishiki = 善知識

a good teacher and friend

よい 先生と
いい おともだち
であえたら
うれしいね

ABOUT THE AUTHOR

John Iwohara
is a Jodo Shinshu priest and author of *Dharma Messages on the Amida-kyo*.

Eri Iwohara
has her illustrations in numerous publications including the *Megumi* magazine.

www.ingramcontent.com/pod-product-compliance
Lightning Source LLC
Chambersburg PA
CBHW061056090426
42742CB00002B/64